The Caring Heart

The Caring Heart

Arlene Stepputat
Paintings by Meganne Forbes

BPB
Blue Point Books

ISBN 1-883423-08-2

First Edition
10 9 8 7 6 5 4 3 2 1

Published by
Blue Point Books
P.O. Box 19347
Santa Barbara, CA 93190
bpbooks@west.net
www.bluepointbooks.com

Printed in China

A portion of the proceeds from the sales of *The Caring Heart* will be donated to the non-profit Heartfelt Foundation in Santa Monica, California. The Heartfelt Foundation, founded in 1978, is a volunteer-driven 501(c)(3) non-profit organization dedicated to serving and assisting people in any form of need.

Heartfelt's mission statement is: "Changing people's lives through the healing power of heartfelt service."

The Heartfelt Foundation can be reached at (310) 829-7857, via email at serve@heartfelt.org or on the Internet at www.heartfelt.org.

When you purchase a copy of *The Caring Heart* you will be giving to charity and demonstrating your own caring heart.

The caring heart is a simple
one. It is open and it is clear.
Complexities have fallen away.
The caring heart awaits
the opportunity to serve.

meganne Forbes

The caring heart listens. There are many distractions in the world and many voices calling. The voice of inner direction is the one to hear, but it is often the softest.

meganne forbes

To hear the inner calling and the answers to life's questions, the caring heart remains still and waits.

The caring heart has faith
and its patience
is its strength.

The caring heart is
a vessel for love.
Compassion fills it.

The caring heart has forgiveness for the past and thus healing for the present.

Letting in the healing power
of giving and receiving
is where the transformation
begins.

The caring heart takes action willingly. It reaches out where pain exists and bears witness. It supports.
It does not ask why.
It simply does whatever is necessary.

The caring heart is courageous. It stands strong in the face of danger or ridicule or judgment.

The caring heart remains vulnerable, even at the risk of being broken.

The heart that serves envisions the changes that are possible. No matter how serious the problem, how much risk is involved, how hopeless and futile it all seems, the caring heart stands firm.

The caring heart is committed to making the vision a reality.

The caring heart is free of
judgment. It is not concerned
with answering all the whys
but with discovering
all the ways.

The caring heart seeks unity
and does not
recognize division.

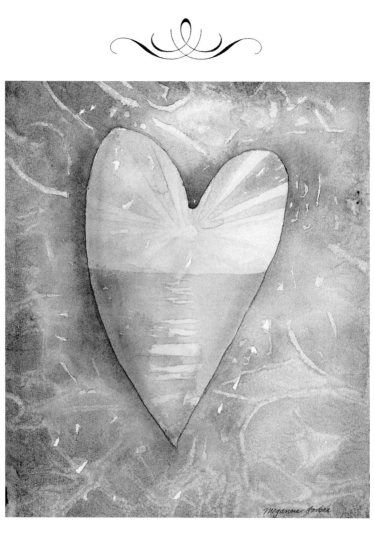

Because the caring heart lives in love's wisdom, it remembers its source. At the core of the caring heart is a flame that also burns in every other heart on the planet.

The caring heart is driven by the power of that connection.

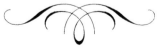

The caring heart recognizes
and serves truth.

Inside each one of us is a caring heart. Finding, acknowledging and living from it is the beginning.

When each one of us lives
in our own caring heart,
we are open, clear,
compassionate and united.
We seek out opportunities to
serve one another in loving.
And that makes
all the difference.

About the Author and *The Caring Heart*

Arlene Stepputat has been involved with community service and volunteerism all her life. She served as Director of Volunteers for Covenant House, New York and led a team of 450 volunteers to national acclaim when the program was recognized by the White House in 1989. Arlene has worked with many organizations to assist them with their own volunteer programs and was a contributing author to the textbook, *The Volunteer Management Handbook*, published by John Wiley and Sons in 1995. Arlene is President of Integrity International, a management and consulting company, as well as a keynote speaker. Arlene also presents workshops and seminars across the United States and abroad.

Arlene conceived and wrote the first draft of *The Caring Heart* in 1990 while taking a personal growth seminar in New York City. She was given twenty-four hours to do something she considered meaningful and important that she had always put off doing. Arlene spent much of that time in St. Patrick's Cathedral writing what would become *The Caring Heart.* She created sixty-five copies of that first version and shared it with her classmates in the seminar and later with friends.

Years later when Arlene met Meganne Forbes, she realized Meganne's lovely paintings perfectly complimented the text of *The Caring Heart.* Arlene continued to refine and polish her book until her message of living together in service and love was crystal clear. One step remained to complete Arlene's vision: the publication of *The Caring Heart.*

With this book the vision has been realized. *The Caring Heart* was made possible by Arlene's husband, Eliot Jacobson, her loving friends, and her publisher, Blue Point Books, who came together to honor Arlene's life-long devotion to loving service. The publication of *The Caring Heart* is their gift to Arlene in honor of her fiftieth birthday. Together they have witnessed the circle of creation, which began as a vision in a place of worship and spirit and was completed in a place of spirit and celebration. Through each of their caring hearts, they have joined together to complete the circle of *The Caring Heart* so that others may learn from it and share Arlene's message throughout the world.

Arlene holds a BA in English from Montclair State University, and MA in Family and Community Education from Columbia University and has equivalent certification in Applied Spiritual Psychology from the University of Santa Monica. She lives in Santa Barbara, California with her husband, Eliot Jacobson, and her loving fur beings, Delta, Camille and Clover.

About the Artist

Meganne Forbes is a watercolor artist living in Carpinteria, California. Her nature-inspired paintings have appeared in many shows in Southern California as well as on book covers, greeting cards and collectors' walls. Meganne paints on handmade paper using the traditional watercolor method.

Meganne describes her painting as a meditation, a time to reflect and be immersed in color and the movement of paint in water. The group of paintings in *The Caring Heart* were born as she let the images happen on their own, watching the watercolor river flow and often being surprised by what occured. Meganne's hope is that the all her paintings bring those who view them joy, relaxation and peace.

During her breaks from painting, Meganne surfs, hikes, spends time with her son, Devon, travels and teaches art. Meganne has a BA in Art from University of California Santa Barbara.

HOW TO ORDER

The Caring Heart

By Arlene Stepputat, Paintings by Meganne Forbes

can be ordered directly from Blue Point Books

VISA®/MASTERCARD® ORDERS CALL TOLL FREE:

1-800-858-1058

or visit our website at **www.BluePointBooks.com**

Each book is **$12.95** including shipping and handling

For information about purchasing our books in quantity
for your company or organization, please contact:

Blue Point Books

P.O. Box 91347, Santa Barbara, CA 93190-1347

805-682-8775

fax: 805-687-0282 • e-mail: bpbooks@west.net

For more about the author, Arlene Stepputat, visit
www.integrity-intl.com.

For more about the artist, Meganne Forbes, visit
www.meganneforbes.com.